BUSINESS OPTIMIZATION STRATEGY SERIES

The Finding, Getting,
Keeping & Growing System

**Stephen Pierce's Business Optimization Strategy Series –
The Finding, Getting, Keeping & Growing System**

Stephen Pierce International, Inc.
101 Washington, # 214
Whitney, Texas 76692
(866) 272-1410

TABLE OF CONTENTS:

Chapter 1: Business Cover Story Review

Your business cover story is your long-term vision for your career. Envision the cover of your favorite magazine. Now, picture yourself on the cover of it. Imagine it's some point in the future, and they have decided to do a complete cover story and feature article on you.

Picture exactly what the headline will read as well as the entire composition of the cover. Imagine the photo used on the cover. Are you standing in front of your home? Are you with your family? Perhaps you're sitting at your office desk.

Now, think of what the feature article entails. Create a hook for the article. It has to be about something substantial you have achieved. Since you are envisioning this, it should be something that you will achieve in the future. Think of where you want your business to go, and what you want to achieve as an individual, and craft your cover story around that.

This feature story holds a business vision theme for your target audience. Take some time to actually create this cover story vision. This exercise is a crucial part of your business realization process. It helps to ground your goals and put you on the path to achieving them.

Feedback on the Process

Our clients have experienced great success from this exercise. One client said:

> ❝ The reason I chose Essence magazine was because of my target audience—more women read that magazine than men. When women read stuff, they talk about stuff. It says, Essence, and right above my picture the title says, 'Dream Maker.' The subtitle says, 'New Voice in Success Helps Transform Lives by Breaking Down Traditional Barriers.' ❞

Another client reported:

> ❝ Some of the big headlines that I had on mine were, 'Success Guru Helps People to Make Their Dreams Become Realities,' 'A 30-year-old Woman Shatters the Shell of Past Abuse and Blossoms into a Vibrant, Energetic Mentor for Abused Teens,' and 'Single Mother of Three Realizes Her Dream of Working from Home and Making Over $70,000 per Year Part-time.'
>
> Another headline I had was different because of my purpose. You had me write up my purpose and it really helped me formulate this: 'Former Teen Gang-Bangers Turn Slum-Ridden Inner City Neighborhood into a Family-Oriented, Clean, Safe Haven.' ❞

When asked insights or feelings that were sparked by the cover story exercise, one student commented:

> ❝ I learned how I wanted to be perceived. I got to the core of what I really wanted, my real intent. The exercise is almost like you passed away and somebody was doing a eulogy, except I'm alive and

they're actually talking about me. I was able to answer the question, 'What do I really want?' My answer was not so much monetary but related to helping others achieve their dreams. Oftentimes, those dreams can't be measured financially. By doing this cover story, I was able to realize that I really want to help people achieve their goals. Whatever dream they have in their heart, it's my goal to try to help and motivate them into achieving that dream. To briefly put it, that's my insight into finding my true focus. **"**

This same student was also asked, "How did it feel while you were doing it and ultimately, how did it feel after you completed the process?" He replied:

" It was kind of frustrating while I was doing it because I was visualizing everything. We had to answer all the individual questions such as, 'What was the photo shoot like?' and 'Who are some of the people around you?' The magazine writers were interviewing some people and asking what they thought about what they learned from me. I felt inspired hearing their stories, more so than if I had been getting the praise myself. **"**

In the process of creating your own future, it's imperative that you are able to visualize it. In order to get from point A to point B, you have to clearly identify both points. The cover story exercise defines your point B—your goal—for you. You also see it in contrast to your point A—where you are right now. You'll then be able to map out the path to achieve your goal.

When we receive feedback from students, it's indicative of the hard work and creativity that goes into the cover story process. Another student described his feature story:

" The headline reads, 'Information Genius Shares Secrets with Others.' There's a photo of Bill and

3

me in our studio, conducting a video seminar to 1,000 eager subscribers who paid $1,000 each for a 90 minute video seminar. The brainstorms are, 'We don't have to develop all the products ourselves. People want to know what the experts know. If you know how to extract this expertise from the experts, you have a product.' My quote is, 'Establish yourself as an authority if you want to attract experts.'

Bill's quote is, 'Just to see if you're paying attention, we just brain-sucked experts and turned the results into products.' The sidebar reads, '(1) Our first information product, (2) Evolution of a future trader and course development, (3) Tele-seminar and podcasting and (4) His new production facility.'

In the article, we share how you decide on an information product as well as how to develop and market it. I featured quotes from us because we've been in Entrepreneur Magazine and Inc.—the usual entrepreneur magazines—but we haven't been on covers. They quoted us or did an article on us but this takes it a step farther. **"**

Take a moment to review your business vision cover story. If you haven't already, write a few quotes that others are saying about you. Remember, this magazine is doing a huge story on you. For example, a possible quote could be, "You helped me turn my expertise into something that's insured my financial security forever."

We asked one student, "What quote would you like to have Oprah say about you in a magazine article?" He replied, "He goes the extra mile. He takes the time to get his head inside your business, and helps you turn that into something that will make you money."

The focus and goals you discover through the exercise serve as "ah-ha" moments for you. After creating her cover story vision, one participant analyzed her overall business plan and described her "ah-ha" moment as:

> ❝ It crystallized that we have to streamline the outsourcing process. We're just starting to get into that because, up until this point for almost all of our products, we've developed them ourselves. We want to reduce the amount of face-time and internal product development required. We already know how to systematize our outsourcing. We know how to do it but we haven't done it. So that's the step-by-step process of doing it. We know that we have to improve our copywriting, list building and conversions. ❞

Do the Work to Reap the Benefits

Completing the exercises is an essential part of the realization process. If you work with a partner or several colleagues, take them through the exercises so they can better understand the company's vision as well as their position in the company.

Through the business cover story process, you'll clearly define your business strengths, weaknesses, opportunities and threats. This not only identifies what you need to grow but also what you need to avoid. The results can be applied to both you individually, and your company.

For your business, the vision cover story solidifies your team and its purpose. Whether you outsource some tasks or keep everything in-house, you should distribute copies of your vision to everyone. Schedule a meeting or teleconference to share your vision cover story with the entire group. They can all then capture your vision. Ask for feedback and aim to implement the good ideas you glean into your cover story. You'll undoubtedly see a more unified team develop since you'll all be on the same page, reaching toward a unified goal.

5

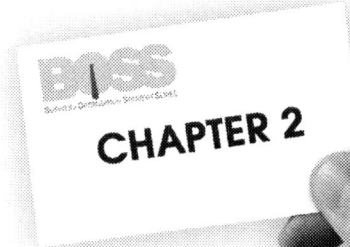

Chapter 2: Focused Strategy

In order to achieve success, you must have a focused strategy in place. Many people have an "intended" strategy—an initial idea of what they want to do. Unfortunately, their focus shifts bit-by-bit until they are way off track from their intended strategy.

This happens when we start to become seduced by other things. There will always be distractions. You have to resist them in order to stay on track towards your goal. If you stay in touch with your driving force, it will keep you on track.

Even if you have a strategy, you'll get off track if you lack your driving force. That force will serve as a solid, unmovable focal point that helps us to develop our business concept and strategic filters. Without that force, you leave the door open to be seduced by other things, and then you just have an intended strategy.

You've likely been in a situation where you have an idea and think, "I'm excited about this idea, and I'm setting out to do it!" Then, all of a sudden, all these other little things start to come in and pull you away from that idea.

The other things might seem to fit initially. They feel good. They cost just the right amount. They feature benefits that seem really good. You then start to gradually shift your focus and spend your time on other things.

Realized Strategy vs. Unrealized Strategy

Unrealized strategy is the ultimate strategy you set out to do. Even though it was your intended strategy, you got off course. Essentially, what you ultimately wanted to do becomes unrealized.

Realized strategy is what you intended to do initially. It'll likely be mixed in with some of the new ideas that were thrown into the strategy. You have to weed out some of those disrupters if they don't belong in your strategy.

Focus is essential. Without it, you will not be able to maintain your journey. Strategy must contain three things:

1. Direction
2. Choice
3. Points of differentiation

When you have a sense of direction, you have your focus. When you have that area of focus, it becomes much easier to choose what you should and shouldn't be doing.

Without a direct course, it becomes extremely difficult to remain focused on the key essentials. If the focus continues to change, you'll never be able to reach your goal. You have to be strong in your focus. It can't change at any given moment, based on what feels right in that instance. There will always be someone trying to sell you on something.

Certain things feel very right in the moment but ultimately they just get you off track. If you look back and take a bird's-eye view, you would see yourself as all over the place. There would be no pattern, consistency, cohesiveness or congruency. Everything would be fragmented, and in retrospect, you can see all the different disrupters coming into play.

When you become focused, you know your driving forces and areas of excellence. Disrupters still come but they are unsuccessful in breaking your focus. This is because you are really clear on what you should and shouldn't be doing.

It's essential to get clear on what you should not be doing. If you don't, then you may think every suggestion is something you should be doing. Your driving force will dictate what you shouldn't be doing. If something doesn't sync up with that driving force, then It's best to stay away from it.

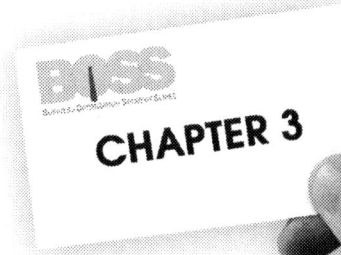

Chapter 3: Mission and Outcome

Your mission is your ultimate goal, and your driving force is the movement that will get you to that goal. As you seek to define both your mission and driving force, you need to ask a few questions:

- Why do we exist?
- Why does this company exist?
- Why does this product exist?
- Why does this service exist?

Those questions will also help define your core values. For example, "As a company, what do we believe in? What core values are going to drive us, helping us to navigate this competitive terrain?"

Your Business Vision

With the cover story vision exercise, you experienced your vision. Part of establishing your vision is asking, "What do we want to be?" As you answer that, you'll get a clear idea on why you exist. When you know what you believe in, you identify the values that are going to help you navigate your course to success.

So, what do you ultimately want to be? Remember, in order to get from point A to point B you must identify both points so that you clearly know your position. If you aren't clear on where you're going, you will undoubtedly end up lost.

When you can identify where you are going and what it will take to get there, you will be able to quickly filter out things that are just not good for you to do. Some of these things that you will have to filter out may, in their own right, be good and exciting; however, they are not right for you at this time.

Remember, just because you *can* doesn't mean you *should*. There are a lot of things you can do but that doesn't mean you should be doing them. You must check in with your mission and driving force before you decide to pursue a particular avenue of thought and action.

Once you have your mission, core values and vision, you'll be ready to develop the foundation of your business. Every part of your business will be built upon this solid foundation.

Developing Your Strategy

In order to establish your strategy, ask yourself these questions:

- What is your ultimate game plan?
- What is the grand strategy for the business?
- What is the grand strategy for this business unit?
- What is the grand strategy for this product?
- What is the grand strategy for this particular service?

If you have a strategy, you can then put into place your measurement systems and implementation. You must measure everything you do. Otherwise, you'll have no gauge for what works. You must also execute and implement your plan with a high degree of concentration and focus.

Again, it's so important to understand that the disruption of strategy exists. Once you have focus, be aware that there will plenty of things that come around to try and break your focus. When you're clear on your direction and choices, you will be able to resist those distractions.

You'll know what differentiates you from your competitors. You'll know what you are, and it won't matter how many distractions show up. No matter how sexy, attractive and seductive those distractions may seem, they won't fit in with your focus. Your strategic filter will just get rid of all those things that don't fit.

As part of your overall strategy, you should develop individual strategic initiatives. These are tasks or mini-goals along the way. Sometimes a particular goal or strategy can be so long-term, it can be difficult to measure progress. When you have these strategic initiatives, your end-goal is more feasible and you can clearly see a tangible track to achieving it.

These individual initiatives should apply to your business as a whole. As a company, team or unit, what must you do to fulfill your mission? What should you do, according to your values, to reach the ideal vision you want to become?

Personal Objectives

You should have your own personal objectives to measure your progress. Ask yourself the question, "What do I need to do?" Make a list of clear, focused things that you must do. Activities can be categorized as meaningful activities versus meaningless activities. Fill your list with meaningful activities.

When you get clear on these different elements, it becomes easy

to understand what you're doing on a day-to-day basis, and whether those daily activities help your ultimate goal.

If something is meaningless, it does not mean it is not important at all. It might be meaningful to somebody or for a particular purpose; however, if it doesn't fit with the ultimate goal, it isn't meaningful to your purpose. To be meaningful, it should contribute to the objectives of the business. It should support your goals, mission, values and vision. If your activities do not align with those objectives, then what you're doing is meaningless to your goal.

Chapter 4: Finding, Getting, Keeping, Growing
- The 4-Phase System -

Regardless of your particular business type, every company has the same challenges when it comes to producing positive results. Whether you're an individual entrepreneur or part of a huge corporation, you will be looking for success in four key areas:

1. Growing your customers
2. Keeping your customers
3. Getting your customers
4. Finding your customers

In the architecture of the 4-Phase System Strategic Map, finding clients is located at the bottom. To download your copy of the 4-Phase System Strategic Map, please go to www.BOSSMembership.com, log into your account and download the worksheet. We then move up to getting clients and eventually keeping clients. Finally, we work our way up to growing clients.

We start at the bottom because before we can get them, we have to find them. Before we can keep them, we have to get them. Before we can grow them, we have to keep them.

The end of one phase is actually the beginning of the next. Once you have found potential customers, you must be beginning to get them as actual customers. Once you have them as customers, you must keep them that way. Finally, once you have kept them as

customers, you must be starting to grow them, thereby expanding their potential and value to your business.

Within systems, every end is the beginning of something else. If it's not the beginning of a new phase, then it's the continuation of the current phase. There is no end to growing clients; it's a continual process.

If you are underperforming profit-wise in your business, you may have driving force issues. Even if you simply have cash flow issues, you must confirm that you know how you're driven as well as your areas of excellence.

Provided you have complete clarity in those areas, your task is then to examine four areas and consider these points:

1. How are you doing in your finding?
2. How are you doing in your getting?
3. How are you doing in your keeping?
4. How are you doing in your growing?

If your company is having profitability problems with your customers, you can look in any four of these areas. You'll begin to find little black holes that you need to close up in order for the company to perform better.

You likely know people who are good at identifying possible customers in the marketplace. Yet they aren't able to get them as customers. They may even identify these potential customers as people that can use their product or service but they aren't able to close the deal.

Perhaps they're really good at closing an initial sale but they have a serious problem keeping customers and making subsequent sales. Due to this huge attrition rate, they are ultimately not successful. Maybe they have a good amount of repeat customers but they can't find a way to get these people to grow. They should be able to grow their customers, making them more valuable to their business by selling them additional products and services.

Use these four phases to examine your business's customer base. You can then find areas within each phase in which you may be lacking. In order to succeed, you must continually be doing all four things: finding customers, getting them, keeping them and growing them. Ideally, you will develop a systematized process where these four strategies are continuously ongoing.

Finding and Getting

We're going to take a moment to look at finding and getting. Under finding and getting, you have demand management which is where you look to create demand. When doing so, you influence a different part of your marketplace and create a different demand.

Remember, when you go into a market, you always have one of two risks. You either have a competitive risk or a demand risk. Competitive risk is present when you enter a marketplace in which there are plenty of competitors. As a result, the question is, "Will you be able to overcome competitive pressures to become successful?"

Demand risk occurs when you enter a market in which there are few or no competitors. You're most likely creating something new. For example, the people who created the DVD player entered a demand risk marketplace. Since there was no such thing as a DVD player before them, they created the demand. The question here is, "How long will this last, and will we be able to maintain it long enough to become successful?"

Demand Management

Everybody has demand management systems which are actually marketing systems. Systems are how profits happen. Proper

marketing systems can actually create demand.

In the finding area, we have to stimulate inquiries. This means you encourage people to inquire for more information, or maybe take a small step in the direction of a purchase. No big jumps happen in the finding area; it's all about small steps forward.

In the getting part, we encourage trial use of our product or service or a small, low-end purchase. This way, we have an opportunity on a completely different level, to build some kind of relationship with them. We can then cultivate and nurture that relationship.

All of this happens on the demand management side, where we put together marketing systems that can eventually run on autopilot. Once we get those marketing systems in place, there's a bit of a systems crossover. This is because selling systems start to take over. Once that happens, supply management comes into play since we've created demand for our product or service.

If you have competitive risk, you need your particular offering to stand out from the competition. You present the customers with a solution to their problem. Your specific offering contributes to their top priorities. Demand management doesn't stop when supply management begins. Instead, you begin to feed the demand with your supply—your products or services.

Keeping and Growing

The customer keeping and growing phases are just as important as the finding and getting phases. For many companies, the sustainability of their profits and growth depend highly on the ability to not only find and get customers but to maintain them over time.

In order to successfully retain customers, you must have a complete selling system in place. This system must take customers through the entire process—from finding and getting them to keeping and growing them. Just like all processes and strategies, you will likely need to continually tweak your system to maximize its performance.

In the keeping area of the customer process, you should encourage repurchase. Remember, when you got them, you offered a trial use of a product or service, or they made a small purchase. Now, in the keeping phase, you want to encourage a purchase of the trial product or service, or repurchase of the initial small purchase.

In the growing phase, you must continue to do those things that grow the value of each individual customer. You should be able to grow and expand their value to the company. It plays an essential part in the continuous process of keeping those customers with your company.

By breaking your business into these four phases, you've created a new model for your company. Now you need to reflect on what you do in your business. Consider a particular activity and ask yourself, "Is this activity part of the finding, getting, keeping or growing phase?" Every activity should be connected to a specific phase. You'll likely find that there are activities you can cultivate in each of these different areas.

Cause and Effect

When you select the proper activities to do in your business, you'll clearly see cause and effect in action. For example, what you do in the finding area should cause something to happen in the getting area. Likewise, what you do in the getting area should cause something to happen in the keeping area. Finally, what you do in the keeping area should cause something to happen in the growing area.

Again, ask yourself, "What are my current key activities in each phase?" The four phases represent the main architecture for success in your business. Remember, every single company has the same challenges of finding, getting, keeping and growing customers. Whether you're a mom-and-pop shop or a huge corporation, the challenge is the same.

In order to profit from this particular architecture, you must have an integrated system that features these different activities. They must be structured in a sequence that drives value to your marketplace. Without that, you will have difficulty succeeding.

4-Phase Questions

As you look at your business in this new framework, there are several questions you should consider. These questions aren't just for this building phase of your business. You should use this framework on a continuous basis to maximize your customer base.

These questions will serve as quick diagnostic tools for your business. You can swiftly assess how you're performing in the areas of profitability and customer value. They serve as a check-in regarding how you are doing in the areas of finding, getting, keeping and growing customers.

1. ***What are your current key activities in each phase?***
   Map out the specific activities in each phase of the process.

2. ***How are you testing, tracking, and measuring results in each phase?***
   For example, in the growing phase, you could have existing customers that you are currently keeping and growing to bring in new customers via referrals.

3. *Which phase is strongest? Why?*

Perhaps you are strong at generating leads, yet when it comes to keeping them, you struggle. This means you excel at the finding and getting phases but wrestle with the keeping and growing phases. You need to analyze why this is the case.

In some instances, your results may be slanted because of how you find and get your customers. Maybe your profit model focuses on those phases but doesn't address the keeping and growing phases.

If so, you may have a transactional mindset. You are constantly thinking of these initial purchases on the front end. As a result, you have a more passive approach to backend selling. This means you don't have a large, sustainable revenue plan. You need to figure out how to actually keep and grow your customers.

In answering this question, you can ask yourself its opposite, "Which phase is the weakest? Why?" You'll then know on which area to focus your attention.

4. *Which activities in each phase produce the best results? Why?*

In order to successfully answer this question, you must have already completely answered question number two. You must have a means of testing, tracking and measuring in order to know which activities in each phase are producing the best results.

5. *Which activities in each phase are producing the worst results?*

This again relates back to question two. You'll know which activities you need to work on if you have accurate tracking of your results.

6. ***What should you do more?***
   Proper measurement allows you to understand where you need to concentrate your focus.

7. ***What should you do less?***
   There may be particular activities on which you are focusing unnecessary time. If something is not producing results, you need to readjust your focus on it. This is all part of the process of optimizing your system.

Every aspect of this process is determined by your driving force. Remember, your driving force defines where you go to find, get, keep and grow your customers. It also dictates what you do to find, get, keep and grow your customers, as well as how you make a profit.

Each area builds off another. You must constantly check in with your driving force. Otherwise, you run the risk of looking to find, get, keep and grow all the wrong people. If you are seeking out customers for the wrong reasons—reasons that don't sync up with your driving force—you can find yourself really stuck.

CHAPTER 5

Chapter 5: FGKG Process in Action

You've now defined all the areas of the 4-Phase model and can now see each phase in action.

In the finding phase, you do something to attract customers to you. In the getting phase, you capture the lead and manage the opportunity. You're interacting with the customer, and participating in a dialogue. You are having some kind of interactive conversation which serves to cultivate and build that relationship.

You want the customer to act on something else. That action can be a purchase or a trial use of your product. Whatever it is, it changes him from a lead to a first-level customer. In some cases, the customer may purchase a small, low-end product but they are more likely to purchase a larger, full product later. The important part is that you've gotten the customer to take action. It's up to you to follow up with him later to maximize that action.

Attract, Interact, Act

Everything has certain patterns and a common pattern always appears in business. For everything you do in business, there are always the patterns of attracting, interacting, and acting. You will see evidence of those patterns within the finding, getting, keeping and growing processes.

When it comes to keeping clients, there are several methods you can employ. First of all, cross-sell; this involves selling multiple products or services to the same client over time.

It may be helpful to put together a system that walks you and your employees through the process. It'll answer specific questions, such as:

- If they don't purchase, then what happens?
- If they don't opt-in, then what happens?
- If they don't take the up-sell, then what happens?
- If they don't take the cross-sell, then what happens?

A complete process map will answer all these questions, addressing each different scene and ensuring proper response systems are in place. You'll have a finite response to each positive or negative activity. Your response will move the customer forward, stall him or move him backwards to an earlier process.

A process map is important because it allows you to easily bring in other people to help you. At that point, you can outsource or employ more people by quickly referring them to your process map.

Take Action

You are an active part of the customer acquisition and retention process. You must take action in order to make it happen. As you take action, you are looking to:

- Build traffic and stimulate inquires
- Encourage trial and purchase
- Encourage repurchase
- Up-sell customers into other programs

The strategic question is, "What are the consistent activities needed to grow profitability?" In each area of finding, getting, keeping and growing, what are the consistent activities needed? Each activity should serve to increase profitability.

After you've found clients, you have to get them and specific activities which go along with that. You have a measurable Most Wanted Response, or MWR, in the getting process. This is what you most want to happen. Ideally, it's some kind of trial or purchase.

In order to get your MWR, you need to have stimulators in place. These stimulators will help you to find, get, keep and grow your perspective. When your vision grows, in turn, your getting process will boom.

In the keeping process, the MWR is a repurchase. The customer is happy, so she stays on and buys from you again.

For the growing process, you should generate word-of-mouth referrals that stimulate your finding process. You can also have up-sell programs in place to make customers more valuable to your business.

Remember, referrals help to lower your costs, saving you advertising and marketing money. They also bring in people with a higher probability of buying. As a result, referrals are incredibly valuable to your company. Customers that refer others to you are doing a high level of business with you. They are gold to your company. Encourage that by making it easy for them to refer others to you. It should be a thoroughly straightforward process for them.

Chapter 6: Marketing Tactic Ideas

There are a multitude of different things you can do to stimulate activity ideas. We've outlined over 100 ways to activate these ideas in the four perspective process. You can download that worksheet at www.BOSSMembership.com. You can brainstorm ideas on your own, or schedule a session with your business team to do so.

There are literally thousands of different things you can do in each perspective– finding, getting, keeping and growing–regarding your customers and clients. This is simply a tactic in your overall strategy.

Ask yourself, "How does this tactic become part of an overall strategy that helps grow every element of my business in each one of those perspectives?" Take a closer look at each one of the perspectives. Figure out how you can use any one of the 124 marketing tactics to get results.

Breakthrough Results

For you to achieve breakthrough results in your business, there are three things that must happen for you to get there:

1. You must describe the strategy.

Articulate and document your strategy. Define it clearly so you and everybody you work with are clear on exactly what it entails. There should be no questions about what you're doing or why you are doing it.

Up until this point, you've spent a lot of time defining why you are doing it. You've also thoroughly covered where you want to ultimately go—your end goals. Now is the time to actually describe the strategy of achieving those goals. Your strategy will serve as your road map.

2. You must measure the strategy.

Measurement is essential. Without it, you won't know how well you are doing. You also won't know if you have gotten off track or off schedule. You must measure in order to judge what works, as well as what does not work. With proper measurement, you'll know how well your strategy is functioning

3. You must manage the strategy.

Manage the strategy on a day-to-day basis continually. Your management will be dictated by the results of your measurements. Check in with daily questions such as, "What are we doing?" and "What do we need to adjust?" You'll never be out of touch with your strategy if you check in with it daily.

If you are disciplined in these three areas, you'll achieve amazing results. If everyone is clear on your strategy, it can be executed. The measurements in place will keep your finger on the health of the strategy. You'll know how the heartbeat of your business is doing at all times. By keeping your finger on that pulse, you'll manage your business's development in the most effective manner possible.

Chapter 7: Strategy

Strategy describes how you intend to create value in each area. Strategy doesn't just relate to your business as a whole. It breaks things down into each phase—finding, getting, keeping and growing.

You must create value in each individual phase. There is value in each phase of the process. Regardless of the size of the desired action, you have to find the value there. Remember, cause and effect relationships are playing between each phase. You must create value in each phase in order for that value to transfer to the next level.

In regard to strategy, competitive advantage comes from both what you do and how you do it. Many people do all of these processes but because they do them incorrectly, they don't get their desired results. This may be because they are continually doing them the same way and expecting different results. If something isn't working, you have to change your approach.

Sometimes it's not about doing things better but rather doing better things. Nobody succeeds on better sameness. Make sure you excel at what you do. Once you're doing well at it, aim to do it better than everybody else. Ideally, you want to move from a point of parody to a point of differentiation.

Creating Value in the Growing Phase

We'll begin at the growing phase and work our way backwards to finding customers. First of all, ask yourself this question, "In order to succeed financially, how should we grow our customers?" As you answer, describe your strategy for creating more value for your existing customers.

We'll assign a keyword to serve as a thought stimulator for your objectives in each of the four areas. Use these keywords:

- Choices
- Personalization
- Customized Services
- Variety

Think of one keyword in regard to a particular phase. How can you use choices to add more value for your existing customers? How can you personalize your products or services to get more referrals? How can you use variety to grow your customers?

Creating Value in the Keeping Phase

For the keeping phase, ask yourself, "To achieve our vision, how will we keep our customers?" Describe the value proposition you're giving to targeted customers and your strategy for retaining those customers.

Since service is a given, your answer can't simply describe service in the great sense. You must get specific in your answer. Don't just think about great customer service but also relationship building. Customer Relationships Management, also known as CRM, is essential to keeping customers. How can you incorporate that into your business to provide better information to your customers?

If you had a CRM system that accumulated details about your customers, you could use that information to better serve them. This would work to help keep them. As a result, you could also provide better service. Customers could call your customer service center and all their details would pop up for the representatives to see. With a clear history of what they've done with your business, questions can be targeted. When a representative asks about a particular instance, the customer feels like he matters to your company.

With such information, a history of the customer's prior purchases, appointments, feedback or event attendance would be easily accessible. You'd have your finger on the heartbeat of every single person because your technology gives you that service edge.

In the keeping stage, think about all these points of service. Consider relationship-based service as a starting point for your value proposition. You can then design the strategy you'll use to keep customers.

Creating Value in the Getting Phase

Ask yourself, "To get our customers, what processes must we master?" It's not enough to just do something; you must excel at it to succeed.

Identify the critical processes that will have the greatest impact on the conversion of leads to customers. Quality is absolutely critical, especially the quality of content and information you provide. If you can demonstrate a history of reliability, perhaps through testimonials, you will be more likely to get customers.

You are looking for ways to convert leads to customers. This process changes someone from a person who might be interested to someone who makes some kind of transaction. What kind of

quality experiences can you demonstrate that motivates leads to convert?

The quality of your products and services can do that but you need to think bigger. How can you package and demonstrate quality? It's better to show rather than simply just tell. Instead of simply verbalizing quality, demonstrate it. You have to actually convert leads if you wish to succeed in business.

Creating Value in the Finding Phase

In the finding phase, just like any phase, customers need to experience, think or assume there will be some level of value. If they don't think that, they won't take whatever action is required, even if that action is as simple as clicking on an online advertisement.

Ask the question, "To achieve our vision, how will we find our customers?" Identify the processes and strategies that are most important to attracting your target customers.

For this finding phase, a trigger word is responsiveness. Focus on channels you can use with a high response rate. You'll find success if you target prospective customers that have a need or desire for what you're offering.

Convenience plays a big part in the finding process. You must make it easy for people. What would make it extremely easy for people to take that first step with you? Speed is another factor. If you can deliver what people want with a fast turn-around time, they will be more likely to take that first step with you.

Timing is another game-changer. Make sure you are in the right place at the right time. Understand that there are seasons to different things, particularly if your offering is related to a specific time of year. For example, if your product is appropriate for

Thanksgiving or Christmas, finding customers in February or March just doesn't make sense. You must figure out how finding customers relates to your overall business schedule.

Consider the methods you use to find customers. Sometimes people use the wrong methods. If you want to use email marketing, it has to be because it is effective for your potential customer base. It cannot be because it is easy. In order to succeed at finding customers, you have got to tap into how your base wants to be contacted.

Barriers to Implementing Strategy

Every business will face barriers to strategy implementation. From single entrepreneurs and mom-and-pop shops to home businesses and mid-sized companies, everyone will face particular challenges.

The first barrier you may encounter is a vision barrier. Statistically, only five percent of people on a team understand the strategy. It is incredibly difficult for people to implement a strategy they don't understand.

Only 10 percent of businesses execute their strategies. We hear the most about those companies that are successful. Yet those companies that outperform the others are all in the top 10 percent of all companies. Those truly exceptional companies with incredible strategies and amazing leadership are in the top one percent of all businesses.

A people barrier is another obstacle. Only 25 percent of managers have incentives linked to strategies. People don't do what you tell them to do; people do what they get paid to do.

If you incentivize people to do something linked to the overall strategy, they will do it. If they know there is a payoff when they

complete the task, they will act. As a result, the strategy is executed and things move forward. Incentives can make a massive difference to your business.

There can also be a management barrier. Eighty-five percent of business teams spend less than one hour per month discussing strategy. Internet entrepreneurs spend a ton of time talking on a tactical level. Though they sometimes think they're discussing strategy, in actuality, they are not.

Finally, you may have resource barriers. Sixty percent of organizations don't link budgets to their overall strategies. Instead, they just complete tasks. If tasks aren't linked in to your whole strategy, they won't help you reach your goal.

Strategy in Action

I recently orchestrated a complete lead generation campaign for a client that took place over one weekend. It started on Saturday morning and went through Sunday until about 2 p.m. The client has a product coming out but he didn't have a prospective customer list for the product. As a result, we needed to generate leads.

I didn't want to just generate general names and email addresses. It took 45 minutes of discussing things with him to come up with a strategy. We generated targeted names, email addresses, full mailing addresses and phone numbers for 5,279 people.

The list we created was strategic, not tactical. There certainly were tactics built into the list but it was all about strategic design. Strategy is extremely powerful.

Another person contacted me for help, and our strategy sessions helped him do $550,000 worth of business in seven days. In fact, we had another strategy session with him because he wanted to re-launch the product.

After his re-launch event, he emailed me and said, "I opened the event at 9 a.m. to the kind of list you told us to develop." This related to the strategy we had put together for him. He wrote, "I did what you said to do, and we sold another hundred units."

In the four hours he had been running the event, he had done another $100,000 in business. It performed better than the initial launch. Our goal was to create a strategy that did better than the first launch. We accomplished that.

Chapter 8: The Planning Process

In the planning process, you have to consider several key points. Vision, objectives, measures, targets and initiatives are the key points you must address.

The first question to ask is, "What are the steps we will be taking to achieve our vision of the future?" Now ask, "What will progress towards our vision of the future look like?" The answers to these two questions cover your vision.

Objectives

Your objectives should be linked to your areas of excellence. Remember, your areas of excellence are directly related to your driving force. If you set objectives that don't really empower the company, then they are useless. You must carve out objectives that match up with your strengths.

If FedEx knows they are distribution driven and they excel at processes, their objectives must link up with those processes. If they don't, it's not going to help them lead the industry. FedEx brought the U.S. Postal Service to its knees. Now you'll find FedEx boxes at all the different post offices. In addition, the U.S. Postal Service uses FedEx to deliver U.S. postal mail. That's what happens with superior strategy.

Set different objectives for the finding, getting, keeping and growing phases. You may have objectives to increase partnering or to build loyalty. Other objectives may include growing revenue, developing customer information or furthering your competencies in different areas. Have proper measures in place so you can manage your achievement.

Let's assume that one of your objectives is to up revenue by increasing up-sells. How will you measure that? You need a base. Suppose 10 percent of people at a particular site take the up-sell. Measure the number of people actually taking the up-sell, and then take steps to target that up-sell.

If you want to increase the up-sell rate to 20 percent, you have a clear objective. You want to double the up-sells to these specific targets. Since you are clear on your objective and your target, you can implement a plan. You can easily measure your progress on a day-to-day basis, based on looking at the number of people taking up-sells.

Initiatives

An initiative is something that goes company-wide. As a company-wide priority, everyone is working to make it happen.

A possible initiative is an add-on program. It could be an operational add-on, with the goal to develop add-on programs that increase your percentage of up-sells on order forms. You could also have a frequency purchase program which will help build customer loyalty. Another initiative could be implementing a CRM system—Customer Relationship Management software— to help you learn more about your customers' buying patterns.

An outsourcing initiative could save you time and money by relegating some work to other providers. An initiative for finding customers could include a partner program. There are all sorts of initiatives you can put in place to help you achieve your goals.

CHAPTER 9

Chapter 9: Apply the Principles to Your Business

You now know the in and outs of the FGKG System—the Finding, Getting, Keeping and Growing System. It's time to apply those principals to your business. Do the homework to apply these to your business.

1. Define an objective for each phase.
2. Identify how you're going to measure that objective.
3. Classify targets.
4. Create an initiative.
5. Execute a plan.

In the real world, you can't simply accumulate information; you must act on it. By creating an actionable agenda for your business, you can reach your goals. Your business will grow as you do the work.

Each piece of work builds on the prior one. One phase is meaningful to the next so it's all part of the greater whole. When you have everything in place, you have objectives, measurements, targets and initiatives. All of which are linked to your areas of excellence that support your driving force.

Ask yourself the key 4-Phase questions, and take time to intricately answer each one. Don't generalize; get specific.

1. What should you do less? Are there activities you should eliminate?
2. What should you do more?
3. What activities should you leave alone?

Define Objectives and Initiatives

Make a full list of all the things you could do. Now, pare this list of objectives down, changing it from what you could do to what you should do. Take it a step further. Examine that list and ask yourself, "On this list of things I should do, what must I do?" You're now narrowing the list down even more, carving it into a must-do list. Finally, strip the list even more, making it the things you will do. Use this clear-cut line of questioning to establish your final list.

- What *could* your objectives be? List a whole bunch of them.
- What *should* your objectives be? Narrow it down.
- What *must* the objectives be? Narrow it down.
- What *will* the objective be?

The final one left is your key objective. Follow this same line of questioning to establish your initiatives.

You must also outline your MTIG triggers—Measures, Targets, Initiatives and Budget. These are real measurement tools you will use to stimulate you in the development process. These triggers will help nudge you in the right direction when you get stuck. Have fun as you establish them.

Your objectives serve as performance objectives, so it's best to start them with action verbs. Use words like increase, reduce, initiate, develop, lower, improve, become and achieve. Try any action verb because you want to articulate and set the objective into motion.

Cover Each Phase

Go through these questions for each phase:

- What is my goal, challenge or problem in finding customers and clients?
- What is the purpose of the solution I'm looking to create?
- Why am I looking to create a solution for this particular area?
- What will creating the solution get me in the areas of finding, getting, keeping and growing customers?

Allow yourself to be stimulated as you work through this assignment. Think about your future. Remember your cover story vision sheet. Tie this work into your overall vision. You will find all sorts of stimulating ideas come your way when you do the actual work.

Continue to ask yourself the key questions: What *could* I do? What *should* I do? What *must* I do? What *will* I do? Then ask yourself, "What is the easiest thing to do first?" This can be a small step in the overall process that can get you going right away.

When you complete this work on each of the four phases, you will become clear on what you should be doing. You'll then have an actionable plan to get it going. From this point forward, you can start to grow your business.

BOSS
BUSINESS OPTIMIZATION STRATEGY SERIES

Ask yourself more key questions in regard to each phase:

- What is limiting me?
- What are my weaknesses?
- What are my threats?
- What is empowering me?
- What are my strengths?
- What are my opportunities?
- Who am I going to be accountable to, and when will this occur?

Now, take these specific answers and apply them to one project you have. Once you apply the answers, it becomes a process. That process then becomes a strategy that can be applied to any project. It sets a foundation for other projects, and eventually it simply becomes a habit. The process provides you with a structured framework to grow your business.

Experimentation Exercises

Revisit your driving forces and experiment with different lines of thinking. For example, if your business were know-how driven, how would it look? Who would your customers and users be? What kind of products and services would you actually create based on your know-how? What industry segments would you actually end up pursuing? What geographical areas would you target?

If you feel you may be driven in another way, do the exact same exercise in that light. Through this experimentation, you'll paint various pictures and one of them will resonant with you. You may discover that you are know-how driven because you know how to serve people. Perhaps you've been serving strictly from your know-how, and now you're ready to take this know-how to the next level. You'll then be leveraging and multiplying it into something greater.

Run different thought experiments and see different scenarios. Keep each experiment in line with your driving forces. You will then come up with ideas that still fit with your overall direction.

Real Results

You can achieve real, tangible results. The intellectual processes are important but we ultimately want tangible results. If you do the work, you'll then be able to go back and look at a documented path of everything you did. You will see how you executed your plan and went from a fuzzy vision to a crystal clear vision. You'll travel from abstract and fragmented actions to concentrated, purposeful and meaningful actions. You'll stretch from random results to consistently growing results.

You have the power to create profits. If you do the work, you can reach your goals.

BOSS
BUSINESS OPTIMIZATION STRATEGY SERIES

BUSINESS OPTIMIZATION STRATEGY SERIES

Notes: